Have I Got a Lie for You!

Get Your Free Gift!

Get a free eBook version of *The Ass Kissers Manual: The Art of Keeping Your Boss Happy!* By Ardemar Gomes and Published by Beckham.

> "…when you are not laughing your butt off, you will be taking notes so that you can perfect the techniques that he so specifically spells out for kissing butt and getting ahead."
>
> --Amazon reader Teresa Mustelier

Subscribe to Beckham Publications Group Updates to get *The Ass Kissers Manual* and special new offers, contests, and more free books.

Paste this url in your browser to sign up:

http://forms.aweber.com/form/73/818584573.htm

HAVE I GOT A
LIE
FOR YOU!

A Fabulous Show Of Donald Trump's Fibs, Fabulations, And Falsehoods

Edited By
Little Man Clarence B. Douglas IV

Introduced By
Two-Legged Mark Twain

Beckham
Publications Group, Inc.

Silver Spring

Published in the United States by
Beckham Publications Group, Inc.
www.beckhamhouse.com
P.O. Box 4066, Silver Spring, MD 20914

ISBN: 978-0-9905904-5-3 eBook
978-0-9905904-6-0 paperback

Library of Congress Control Number:
2016938545

Critical Raves!

"If you tell a big enough lie and tell it frequently enough, it will be believed."

— Adolf Hitler

"He who permits himself to tell a lie once, finds it much easier to do it a second and third time, till at length it becomes habitual."

–Thomas Jefferson

"There is no vice that doth so cover a man with shame as to be found false and perfidious."

–Francis Bacon

"A good man will not lie, although it be for his profit."

–Cicero

"O, what a tangled web we weave; When first we practice to deceive!"

–Sir Walter Scott

"False words are not only evil in themselves, but they infect the soul with evil."

–Plato

"He who tells a lie, is not sensible how great a task he undertakes; for he must be forced to invent twenty more to maintain that one."

–Alexander Pope

"A liar will not be believed even when he speaks the truth."

–Aesop

Contents

Acknowledgments

My United Kingdom-based research assistant, Mari was instrumental in the research effort and deserves credit for her speedy and accurate accumulation of facts.

I thank especially the following networks, web sites, newspapers and writers whose investigative work made tracking down the truth markedly easy.

CNN
FactChek
FindLaw
Huffington Post
Mother Jones
Pew Research Center
Politico
Siena College poll
ThinkProgress
USA Today/Suffolk University poll

Wall Street Journal
Washington Post
Washington Post-Univision poll
WSJ/NBC poll
Lauren Carroll
Kevin Drum
Rosalind S. Helderman
Warren Fiske and Louis Jacobson
Scott Keyes

Eugene Kiely

Tal Kopan and
Elise Labott

Ephrat Livn

Nick Niedzwiadek

Karl Rove

Gary Tuchman

Introducton

On The Decay of The Art of Lying
by Mark Twain

OBSERVE, I do not mean to suggest that the *custom* of lying has suffered any decay or interruption—no, for the Lie, as a Virtue, a Principle, is eternal; the Lie, as a recreation, a solace, a refuge in time of need, the fourth Grace, the tenth Muse, man's best and surest friend, is immortal, and cannot perish from the earth while this Club remains.

My complaint simply concerns the decay of the *art* of lying. No high-minded man, no man of right feeling, can contemplate the lumbering and slovenly lying of the present day without grieving to see a noble art so prostituted.

In this veteran presence I naturally enter upon this scheme with diffidence; it is like an old maid trying to teach nursery matters to the mothers in Israel. It would not become me to criticize you, gentlemen, who are nearly all my elders—and my superiors, in this thing —and so, if I should here and there *seem* to do it, I trust it will in most cases be more in a spirit of admiration than I.

No fact is more firmly established than that lying is a necessity of our circumstances —the deduction that it is then a Virtue goes without saying. No virtue can reach its highest usefulness without careful and diligent cultivation—therefore, it goes without saying that this one ought to be taught in the public schools—at the fireside—even in the newspapers.

What chance has the ignorant, uncultivated liar against the educated expert? What chance have I against Mr. Per—against a lawyer? *Judicious* lying is what the world needs. I sometimes think it were even better and safer not to lie at all than to lie injudiciously. An awkward, unscientific lie is often as ineffectual as the truth.

Now let us see what the philosophers say. Note that venerable proverb: Children and fools *always* speak the truth. The deduction is plain—adults and wise persons never speak it. Parkman, the historian, says, "The principle of truth may itself be carried into an absurdity." In another place in the same chapter he says, "The saying is old that truth should not be spoken at all times; and those whom a sick conscience worries into habitual violation of the maxim are imbeciles and nuisances."

It is strong language, but true. None of us could *live* with an habitual truth-teller; but, thank goodness, none of us has to. An habitual truth-teller is simply an impossible creature; he does not exist; he never has existed.

Of course there are people who *think* they never lie, but it is not so—and this ignorance is one of the very things that shame our so-called civilization. Everybody lies—every day; every hour; awake; asleep; in his dreams; in his joy; in his mourning; if he keeps his tongue still, his hands, his feet, his eyes, his attitude, will convey deception— and purposely.

If a stranger called and interrupted you, you said with your hearty tongue, "I'm glad to see you," and said with your heartier soul, "I wish you were with the cannibals and it was dinner-time." When he went, you said regretfully, *"Must* you go?" and followed it with a "Call again"; but you did no harm, for you did not deceive anybody nor inflict any hurt, whereas the truth would have made you both unhappy.

I think that all this courteous lying is a sweet and loving art, and should be cultivated.

The highest perfection of politeness is only a beautiful edifice, built, from the base to the dome, of graceful and gilded forms of charitable and unselfish lying.

What I bemoan is the growing prevalence of the brutal truth. Let us do what we can to eradicate it. An injurious truth has no merit over an injurious lie. Neither should ever be uttered. The man who speaks an injurious truth, lest his soul be not saved if he do otherwise, should reflect that that sort of a soul is not strictly worth saving. The man who tells a lie to help a poor devil out of trouble is one of whom the angels doubtless say, "Lo, here is an heroic soul who casts his own welfare into jeopardy to succor his neighbor's; let us exalt this magnanimous liar."

An injurious lie is an uncommendable thing; and so, also, and in the same degree, is an injurious truth—a fact which is recognized by the law of libel.

Among other common lies, we have the

silent lie— the deception which one conveys by simply keeping still and concealing the truth. Many obstinate truth-mongers indulge in this dissipation, imagining that if they *speak* no lie, they lie not at all.

Lying is universal—we *all* do it; we all *must* do it. Therefore, the wise thing is for us diligently to train ourselves to lie thoughtfully, judiciously; to lie with a good object, and not an evil one; to lie for others' advantage, and not our own; to lie healingly, charitably, humanely, not cruelly, hurtfully, maliciously; to lie gracefully and graciously, not awkwardly and clumsily; to lie firmly, frankly, squarely, with head erect, not haltingly, tortuously, with pusillanimous mien, as being ashamed of our high calling.

Then shall we be rid of the rank and pestilent truth that is rotting the land; then shall we be great and good and beautiful, and worthy dwellers in a world where even benign Nature habitually lies, except when she promises execrable weather. Then— But I am but a new and feeble student in this gracious art; I cannot instruct *this* Club.

Joking aside, I think there is much need of wise examination into what sorts of lies are best and wholesomest to be indulged, seeing we *must* all lie and *do* all lie, and what sorts it may be best to avoid —and this is a thing which I feel I can confidently put into the hands of this experienced Club—a ripe body, who may be termed, in this regard, and without undue flattery, Old Masters.

This is an abridged version of the essay delivered by Mark Twain at the meeting of the Historical and Antiquarian Club of Hartford, Connecticut in 1885.

Fibs

Made-up stories and details, scuttlebutt, neighborhood rumors, inventions like those created by children

---

Trump "heard" that Obama is "thinking about signing an executive order where he wants to take your guns away."

Reportedly, Obama considered a requirement that high-volume private gun dealers conduct background checks.

Trump said he heard that the Obama administration had plans to accept 200,000 Syrian refugees—and in a later speech increased that number to 250,000.

The number is about 10,000.

Trump said in June, 2015, "There are no jobs" to be had.

Official statistics revealed 5.4 million job openings—the most in 15 years.

Claims Trump, "The Mexican government ... they send the bad ones over."

No evidence shows that the Mexican government inspires criminals to cross the border. Recent statistics reveal that show illegal immigration from Mexico dropped off dramatically during the 2008-2009 recession and has remained low.

He said that 13 Syrian refugees were "caught trying to get into the U.S."

They walked up and requested asylum, knowing that to enter the United States looking for refugee status, they must go through a strict application process.

Trump claimed that the United States sends to Japan "like nothing, by comparison, nothing."

The United States exported $62 billion in goods to Japan in 2015, according to Politico.

Trump said, "One of the polls just came out, and a number of them have just come out. I'm beating Hillary Clinton quite easily, thank you."

That week some polls showed him two points ahead of Clinton while others showed she'd beat him.

Trump says that many people saw pipe bombs sitting around the house of the San Bernardino shooters but said nothing to police.

No evidence supports or verifies his claim.

He won't run as a third party candidate, declaring, "I will endorse the 2016 Republican presidential nominee regardless of who it is. I further pledge that I will not seek to run as an independent or write-in candidate nor will I seek or accept the nomination for president of any other party."

On a Sunday after this proclamation, Trump told ABC's George Stephanopoulos that he remains open to a third-party run.

Trump criticized the May 2014 exchange of Army Sgt. Bowe Bergdahl, held by the Taliban, for five Guantanamo Bay detainees "They're back on the battlefield, trying to kill everybody, including us," he declared, referring to the released Taliban members.

Each of those released detainees remained under government surveillance in Qatar, a U.S. ally.

In the September GOP presidential debate, Trump said, "We don't get along with the heads of Mexico."

Mexico is our country's third largest trade partner, and its president has praised President Obama on several fronts, including immigration.

He asserted that under Obama, income and employment for African-Americans is "worse than just about ever."

Black income and employment has historically been proportionately less than whites' for most of the last 50 years. They have improved during the Obama presidency.

Trump proclaimed that Vermont Senator Bernie Sanders would tax "you people" at a 90 percent rate.

Sander's own plan, although not then specified, is around 50 percent for the country's wealthiest earners.

Trump said that 61 percent of our bridges are in danger of falling.

According to the Federal Highway Administration's latest available accounting, about 10 percent are structurally deficient.

Trump claims that the police are the most mistreated people in this country.

Statistics show that groups like gay and transgender youth are far more often mistreated.

Trump claims that climate change is a hoax invented by the Chinese.

Scientists, not the Chinese, describe the rising levels of carbon dioxide and other heat-trapping gases in the atmosphere that have warmed the Earth. The impacts are plentiful, including rising sea levels, melting snow and ice, more extreme heat events, fires and drought, and more extreme storms, rainfall and floods. Researchers say that these trends will continue and likely accelerate, posing significant risks to human health and other natural resources.

Trump calculates that America has the highest tax rate in the world.

The top income tax rate in the United States is 39.6 percent, ranking it 33rd highest on a list of the top rates in 116 nations compiled by international tax advisory corporation KPMG.

Trump maintained that the Iran deal forces us to "fight with Iran against Israel" if Israel attacks Iran.

Secretary of State John Kerry testified before Congress that nothing about the provision—Section 10 of Annex III of the deal, which covers civil nuclear cooperation—compels the U.S. to side with Iran against any attack.

Fabulations

Made-up, myth-like fairy tale stories told by boasters, show-offs, and self-publicists

Trump said that his tax plan is revenue neutral.

According to Tax Foundation estimates, his plan would reduce revenues to the U.S. Treasury by more than $10 trillion over 10 years.

Trump described a two-year old who got autism a week after the child received a vaccine.

There's no evidence of a link between vaccines and autism.

Trump claimed credit for getting Ford Motor Co. to move a plant from Mexico to Ohio.

Ford *hasn't* changed its plans to build new $2.5 billion facilities in Mexico.

On March 8, 2016, Trump declared that a trade deficit with Japan was over $100 billion a year.

The deficit was about $69 billion.

He said that support for abortion is going down.

Approval of legal abortion jumped from 51 percent to 58 percent between January and December 2015, according to the Associated Press-GFK Poll.

Trump says that Republicans wouldn't even be talking about illegal immigration were it not for him.

Immigration has been a central Republican Party issue for decades before Trump became a candidate.

He watched on television as "thousands and thousands" of Muslims in New Jersey were "cheering" the fall of the World Trade Center on Sept. 11, 2001.

No news organizations nor the New Jersey attorney general's office could find evidence of these public celebrations during the 9/11 attack.

He accused New York City Mayor Bill de Blasio of being "the worst mayor in the United States. I hate watching what is happening with dirty streets, the homeless, and crime!"

New York City is one of the safest major cities in the world, and the safest in America. Crime rates are down although homelessness is rising.

Warns Trump, "The migration, they're coming across. Obama wants to bring thousands and thousands of people in. He has no idea who they are."

No proposal has been made to accept refugees without screening them for security, although the process is considered far too time-consuming.

About Florida Senator Marco Rubio, Trump declares, "He's totally in favor of amnesty."

Rubio did not propose blanket amnesty but did co-sponsor a bill that included a way to citizenship.

Trump whined, "Really they've shut Christianity down."

Seven in 10 Americans identify as Christian, according to the Pew Research Center.

Trump announced, "I'm not going to take any money. I don't want any money…You know, I've self-funded my campaign….Right now, I'm into, you would know better than me, maybe $30 million, maybe more."

By then, the end of January 2016, his campaign had accepted $7.5 million from donors not named Donald J. Trump. Trump gave his campaign $250,318 and lent $17.5 million that is repayable at any time until shortly after the election.

Trump announced in March, "I have not even focused on Hillary yet…I haven't even started with her other than four weeks ago."

Months earlier, in December, Trump had declared that Clinton's bathroom break during a Democratic debate was "disgusting" and that Barack Obama "schlonged" her in the 2008 primaries.

"Little Marco Rubio," began Trump, "you know, he's a no-show in the U.S. Senate. He never goes to vote."

Rubio missed 229 of 1,517 votes between January 2011 and March 2016, or 15 percent. The median record for missed votes for senators currently serving is 1.7 percent.

Trump bragged, "Wasn't that funny last night when Cruz said, I'm the only one that can beat Donald Trump. I have demonstrated that I can beat him. I won five states."

Cruz correctly said at that point that he had won eight states, not five.

Boasted Trump in March, "One of the polls just came out, and a number of them have just come out. I'm beating Hillary Clinton quite easily, thank you."

A *USA Today*/Suffolk University poll for mid-February showed him two points ahead of Clinton, but most of the polls showed her beating him.

In March, Trump trumped, "After Paris, all of a sudden it started changing. We started getting polls in. And everybody liked Trump from the standpoint of ISIS, from the standpoint of the military."

After the Paris attacks, According to a *Washington Post*-ABC poll, only 42 percent of GOP respondents assessed Trump as the best candidate to handle the threat of terrorism.

Boasted Trump in March, "They do a poll in South Carolina, Lindsey Graham endorses somebody else and the poll in South Carolina has me at 47 percent."

Trump never topped 42 percent in all the polls collected by sources like Real Clear Politics. He won the state with 32.5 percent of the vote.

Trump declared, "Upstate New York I poll higher than anybody ever."

According to a Siena College poll, Hillary Clinton would beat Trump 56 percent to 33 percent in upstate New York. It predicted that the only region in New York that he would win is in the state's suburban areas—by five points.

Trump criticized Obama's "excessive" use of executive orders, saying American government is "not supposed to work that way."

President Obama has issued fewer executive orders than either Bill Clinton, George W. Bush, or Ronald Reagan.

"They," roared Trump, "had me practically dying in South Carolina the day before…and it looked like I was really in trouble and then I won in a landslide. The poll was wrong."

It wasn't a landslide since that South Carolina NBC/*WSJ* poll showed Trump at 28 percent versus Texas Senator Mario Cruz at 23 percent. A national *WSJ*/NBC poll showed Cruz ahead of Trump by 28 percent to 26 percent.

Trump reported in March, "Then all of a sudden the *WSJ*/NBC come up with this poll that was very close. They put it on the front-page of the *Wall Street Journal*, front-page. They never do that...I never do well in the *Wall Street Journal* polls; it's set against me."

The Journal customarily covers polls on its front page, showing Trump in favorable positions in many stories. A headline from mid-January announces, "Poll: Donald Trump Widens His Lead in Republican Presidential Race."

He claimed, "We're winning every poll with the Hispanics."

Eighty percent of registered Hispanic voters view Trump unfavorably, reported a February *Washington Post*-Univision poll.

Boasts Donald Trump, "I built an unbelievable, some of the greatest assets in the world, very little debt, tremendous cash flow, tremendous. Almost all of my businesses work."

At least three of Trump's companies have declared bankruptcy, primarily because they could not repay their debts.

The Trump Plaza Hotel declared bankruptcy in 1992 with $550 million in debt.

The Trump Hotels and Casinos Resorts filed for bankruptcy in 2004 carrying an estimated $1.8 billion in debt.

In December 2008, Trump Entertainment Resorts couldn't pay a $53.1 million interest payment for a bond.

Declared Trump, "I don't settle lawsuits… I don't do it."

In 2016, Trump settled the lawsuit with Univision Communications Inc. after the Spanish-language network refused to air the Miss USA pageant based on his disparaging remarks about Mexicans.

In 2013, Trump settled with condo buyers who had sued over a project in Baja California.

The US Department of Justice sued Trump successfully for antitrust violations in 1988, and he settled the suit for $750,000.

In 1983, the Local 95 Pension sued Trump in federal court for defrauding workers out of benefits funds contributions by employing non-union laborers. The case ended in a sealed settlement.

Complained Trump, "The only way, now everybody's talking about how massive these crowds are, the only way they find out about the crowds, the only way is with the protestors."

The media has consistently noted the size of Trump's audiences with or without protestors. As an example, CNN covered Trump's August 2015 crowd of 30,000 at an Alabama football stadium.

Trump says that we still "really don't know" if Barack Obama was born in the United States.

President Barack Hussein Obama was born on the island of Oahu in Hawaii at 7:24 p.m. on August 4, 1961, according to his birth certificate that is "absolutely authentic," according to Dr. Chiyome Fukino, a former director of the Hawaii Department of Health. "He was absolutely born here in the state of Hawaii," she told CNN.

Falsehoods

Deliberately and knowingly misstating facts, lying

He predicted Osama bin Laden.

His *Trump: The Art of the Deal* mentioned bin Laden once, and didn't predict anything about bin Laden's upcoming plans.

Trump said that he got to know Vladimir Putin "very well" while the two were on CBS' "60 Minutes."

They were interviewed separately, while thousands of miles apart in different countries.

He claimed that his campaign is 100-percent self-funded.

Trump's campaign raised about $19.4 million by the end of 2015, and he contributed almost $13 million of that himself. Most of the balance came from individual contributions.

Trump said Mexico doesn't have a birth right citizenship policy.

It does. Mexican nationality is obtained by birth if the person is born within the republic's territory, regardless of whatever the parents' nationality is.

He denied that he ever called female adversaries "fat pigs, dogs, slobs and disgusting animals."

He called comedian Rosie O'Donnell a "big, fat pig," and "you take a look at her, she's a slob."

Huffington Post Editor Arianna Huffington: "A dog who wrongfully comments on me."

Elizabeth Beck, a lawyer who requested a break from a deposition to pump breast milk: "'You're disgusting, you're disgusting."

Trump claimed economic growth in the U.S. has "never" been below zero—until the third quarter of 2015. "Who ever heard of this?"

Economic growth has been below zero 42 times since 1946.

Trump shared an image on Twitter showing "Whites killed by whites: 16%. Whites killed by blacks: 81%.

The number of whites killed by whites was 82 percent in 2014, and the number of whites killed by blacks was 15 percent.

In Concord, New Hampshire, Trump declared, "We're losing our jobs and the politicians don't tell you that."

The U.S. Department of Labor reported recently that the country is at its lowest unemployment rate since February, 2008.

On March 11 in St. Louis, Trump stated, "We don't win at trade. We lose to everybody at trade."

The United States in 2015 had trade surpluses with countries that include Hong Kong, the Netherlands, the UAE and Australia.

Trump declared, "Remember we used to have Made in the USA, right? When was the last time you've seen it? You don't see that anymore."

In 2014, The U.S. Economics and Statistics Administration reported that U.S. manufacturers sold $4.4 trillion of goods that classify as Made in the U.S.A.

The National Association of Manufacturers detailed that manufacturing contributes $2.17 trillion to the U.S. economy and employs 12.3 million Americans.

Trump claimed that health care is "going up 35, 45, 55 percent."

Since President Obama has been president, premiums rose an average of 5.8 percent a year, compared to 13.2 percent in the previous nine years.

Trump declared, "I've spent the least money and I'm by far number one. So I've spent the least."

Trump's campaign had spent $23.9 million by February 2016, more than Ohio Gov. John Kasich's campaign, which had spent $7.2 million, or $19.5 million including money from outside groups supporting him.

Trump said that he's self-funding his campaign, and he was "not taking money...I spent a lot of money. I don't take." He also declared: "Right now, I'm into, you would know better than me, maybe $30 million, maybe more."

By then, according to Politico, Trump had solicited donations on his campaign website, and accepted $7.5 million in donations. Trump had given his campaign $250,318, and lent another $17.5 million to it.

Trump claimed that $50 million of negative ads were targeted against him in Florida, and "So many horrible, horrible things said about me in one week. $38 million worth of horrible lies."

Outside groups had spent $15 million in Florida before the week of that statement, according to Politico. Moreover, every GOP dollar not spent by Trump on TV and radio in the March week amounted to $10.57 million, according to The Tracking Firm, which monitors media buys. And not all of that money was negative against Trump.

Trump said that families of the Sept. 11, 2001, hijackers had been living in the U.S. before that date. "The wife knew exactly what was happening. They left two days early ... and they watched their husband on television flying into the World Trade Center, flying into the Pentagon."

No relatives of the 9/11 hijackers had been living in the U.S. before the attacks. Osama bin Laden's family members, who were not known to have forewarning of the attack, were evacuated by

Saudi Arabia's government nine days later for their safety.

Trump refused to disavow former Ku Klux Klan leader David Duke, declaring three times, "I don't know anything about David Duke."

During a Bloomberg interview in August 2015, Trump was considering running for president as a Reform Party candidate and named Duke as a cause for concern. "Well, you've got David Duke just joined—a big racist, a problem. I mean, this is not exactly the people you want in your party," he said.

Footage from one of Trump's campaign ads shows dozens of people climbing over a border fence and the narrator says, "He'll stop illegal immigration by building a wall on our southern border that Mexico will pay for."

The footage was shot 5,000 miles away in Morocco and aired May 3, 2014, on Italian television.

Trump criticized the May 2014 exchange of Army Sgt. Bowe Bergdahl, held by the Taliban, for five Guantanamo Bay detainees "They're back on the battlefield, trying to kill everybody, including us," he declared, referring to the released Taliban members.

Each of those released detainees remained under government surveillance in Qatar, a U.S. ally.

After a mass shooting at Umpqua Community College in Oregon, Trump described the school as a "gun free zone."

Anyone with a valid concealed carry license is allowed to have a gun on the campus.

Trump claims that the 14th Amendment says that babies born to illegal immigrants inside the U.S. are not citizens.

The amendment states that all persons born in the United States are citizens of the United States and of the state wherein they reside.

Trump said that his book *Trump: The Art of the Deal* is the best-selling business title of all time.

Industry reports show sales of one million since publication.

The 7 Habits of Highly Effective People has sold almost 25 million, *How to Win Friends & Influence People* has sold 15 million copies, and *Rich Dad Poor Dad* has sold four million.

Trump blamed the Paris terror attacks on too few guns in civilian hands, and that Paris has "the strictest no-gun policy of any city anywhere in the world."

France ranks 12 on the list of most guns per capita in the world. Many French civilians own guns.

Trump said that the Obamacare website doesn't work.

The site had maintenance problems in the days after its launch, but it's working today, and millions of Americans have signed up there for insurance plans under the Affordable Care Act.

Trump claimed that the GDP (gross domestic product) shrank under Obama at the beginning of 2015 and that "it's never under zero."

The GDP grew in the beginning of 2015, and during recessions it does shrink.

Trump announced that if "you look at the jobs reports, which are totally phony, because if you stop looking for a job you are essentially considered employed."

Discouraged workers who stop looking for a job leave the workforce. So they don't count toward unemployment. But they don't count as employed either.

Trump harrumphed, "I know there are some companies where the people were full time for 25 years. Now they're part-timers and they go out and get another job, and that has to do solely with Obamacare."

The trend of Americans increasingly changing jobs more often and working on a part-time basis far predates Obamacare.

Trump heralded, "Countries have lobbyists also. They have lobbyists. They have their donors."

Under the U.S. Foreign Agents Registration Act, foreign nationals are not allowed to contribute to political campaigns.

Trump proclaimed, "Ohio got lucky because they struck oil. And the budget of Ohio went up more than any budget in the entire United States."

Ohio's budget rose from $55.9 billion in 2010 to $64 billion in 2015, but North Dakota's increase was greater, and New York's was higher in dollar terms, based on National Association of State Budget Officers' data.

Trump announced that ISIS drowns "people in these massive steel cages where 40, 50, 60 people they dump it and they pull it up half an hour later with 50 people dead."

In June, ISIS released a video featuring the group drowning of five Iraqis in a cage. No reports exist of 40 to 60 victims drowning.

Trump declares that he opposed the Iraq War and has dozens of news clippings to prove it.

No newspaper archives or TV transcripts show that he publicly opposed the war before it began in March 2003.

He will allow guns at Trump golf resorts.

Managers at most of his hotels and golf courses reported to ThinkProgress that the locations are gun-free zones, even for guests with concealed-carry permits.

Trump maintained that people on the terrorism watch are already prohibited from buying guns.

In December 2015, the Senate turned aside a measure that would prohibit suspected terrorists from buying guns.

Donald Trump proclaimed insisted that ISIS built a luxury hotel in the Middle East.

The Islamic State reopened the five-star Ninawa International Hotel in Mosul that shut down when the terrorist group took over the city, one of the largest in

Iraq. So the Islamic State just occupied the Ninawa International Hotel. They didn't build it.

Trump declares that he was never interested in opening a casino in Florida.

The *Washington Post* reports that documents and interviews prove that Trump tried to get casino gambling in Florida during Governor Jed Bush's term. He had donated to the state GOP and held meetings with house speaker John Thrasher and other state officials. Reportedly Bush said, "I'm not going to be bought by anybody."

According to Trump in November, 2015, The United States only started bombing ISIS oil fields "two days ago."

The U.S. had been conducting limited airstrikes called Operation Inherent Resolve against the terrorist group's oil infrastructure since August 2014, and intensified attacks when it launched Operation Tidal Wave II in October 2015.